Jackie and the Pony Rivals

Jackie and the misfit Pony

Jackie and the Pony Rivals

Judith M. Berrisford

Illustrated by Geoffrey Whittam

HODDER AND STOUGHTON
LONDON   SYDNEY   AUCKLAND   TORONTO

For Anna-Kristina, Caroline, Zoe and Justin Bell; Jeremy, Peggy and Patricia O'Caroll; Rachel and Mark Le-Pine Williams for having such wonderful grandparents as Basil and Anne.

Berrisford, Judith Mary
  Jackie and the pony rivals.
  I. Title
  823'.9'1J   PZ7.B4614

  ISBN 0–340–25206–5

Typesetting by King's English Typesetters Ltd., Cambridge. Printed in Great Britain by St. Edmundsbury Press, Bury St. Edmunds, Suffolk for Hodder and Stoughton Children's Books, a division of Hodder and Stoughton Ltd, Mill Road, Dunton Green, Sevenoaks, Kent TN13 2YJ.

Contents

1 Disaster – plus Rob

'Look! There's the loch. It can't be much further to the pony farm.'

My cousin Babs craned forward to gaze through the windscreen of the horse-box at the attractive Scottish countryside ahead.

There were five of us on the front seat – Babs, her school-friend, Fiona, Fiona's aunt Mrs Duncan (who owned the pony stud), my golden cocker spaniel Scamp, and me.

In the back were Babs' skewbald pony, Patch, and my grey, Misty. 'Yes, we'll be at Lochside in less than five minutes,' Mrs Duncan confirmed, glancing at her wrist-watch. 'Just in time for lunch.'

I'm a bit hazy about what happened next. I think Babs had said something about how kind it was of Mrs Duncan to let Fiona invite Babs and me and our ponies to have a holiday at the pony farm. Then there was a sudden bang from beneath the horse-box as one of the tyres burst. Luckily, we weren't going fast because the road was little more than a stony track amid the heather.

'Blow out!' Mrs Duncan exclaimed as the horse-box wobbled off-course.' 'Don't panic!' She steered into the

7

wobble and slowly applied the brake. 'Everything's under control.'

In another minute, she would have safely pulled up, but the sun was in her eyes and so she probably didn't notice a big stone in the rough road ahead. The front off-side wheel went over it with a bump and the other front wheel ploughed into a deep rut.

The horse-box lurched sideways, squashing us all together in the cab. From behind, Misty and Patch began to squeal, frightened.

I held my breath, expecting us to crash right over and to roll down the hillside. Then, the miracle happened!

The tilt of the horse-box was stopped at an angle of about forty-five degrees as it came to rest against the trunk of a stout hawthorn growing beside the road.

'Gosh! That was a near thing!' Fiona's voice sounded shaken. 'How on earth are we going to get out?'

'Easy!' Babs managed to force the near-side door open and she and I slid out, to hurry to the back of the horse-box and rescue our ponies.

I knelt down while Babs stood on my back to reach the bolts. Then the ramp came clattering down and we had to move quickly to get out of the way.

When the door was open our ponies could see that the world outside the tilting box was reassuringly normal and Misty and Patch quickly recovered from their fright. They were more puzzled than scared as they stood in the V formed by the tilting floor and the

side of the horse-box. They had straw in their manes.

'Come on, Misty!' I coaxed my pony.

Hooves slipping on the sloping floor, Misty tucked up her fore-legs and jumped neatly from the van. Patch followed.

For a moment, both ponies looked around, snuffing the salty air blowing up from the sea-loch, before they dropped their heads to graze.

'Babs! Jackie!' Fiona's voice from the cab of the horse-box was followed by an anxious whining from Scamp.

'What is it, Fiona? Why don't you and your aunt get out?' I hurried to the door of the cab which was still swinging open. 'Come on! Are you shaken? Let me give you a hand.'

'It's not me,' said Fiona. 'It's Aunt Isabel. I think she must somehow have knocked her head in the crash. She's blacked out.'

Scrambling into the cab, Babs and I gazed across Fiona to Mrs Duncan. Her eyes were shut. Her face was pale. She seemed to be breathing heavily, and, in spite of Scamp licking desperately at her face in an attempt to rouse her, she did not move.

'She seems to have fainted,' said Fiona.

'Not fainted,' I said with memories of first-aid lessons at school. 'I think she's concussed.'

'So do I,' agreed Babs. 'We mustn't move her. You stay with your aunt, Fiona, while Jackie and I ride down to the house and telephone for a doctor.'

'Don't leave me on my own.' Fiona looked scared. 'Suppose Aunt Isabel came round. I wouldn't know what to do . . .'

'Of course you would!' said Babs 'Don't you remember what we learned in first aid?'

'It's gone right out of my head.' Fiona's face was pale. She caught at Babs' sleeve. 'Aunt Isabel's going to be all right, isn't she? I mean, she isn't going to die or anything?'

'Of course not!' Babs sighed impatiently. 'Well, if you're going to be such a scared duck, Fiona, I suppose I'd better stay here with you.'

'And I'll take Misty and gallop down to Lochside.' Sliding out of the cab, I ran to the back of the

10

horse-box to collect Misty's bridle and saddle. A few minutes later we were galloping down the heathery hill-side towards the old grey farm-house by the loch where Fiona's widowed aunt lived with her fifteen-year-old son, Rob, and their stud of Highland ponies.

Rob must have heard Misty thundering over the heather because he came to the farm-yard gate to meet us. He gave a baffled smile and I realised that he had been expecting the horse-box with his mother, Fiona and Babs as well. The hazel eyes beneath his thatch of curly, dark hair were nonplussed as he saw only me.

He must have noticed my wild and worried look, however, because his smile faded and he became instantly alert.

'Something's wrong, isn't it?' he asked quickly. 'Tell me what.'

'Don't be too alarmed,' I began. 'The horse-box left the road. Your mother's knocked her head. I expect she's concussed. We ought to get a doctor.'

'Right!'

Rob did not let the shock of the news stop him acting immediately. He ran into the house. Through the hall doorway I saw him pick up the telephone.

A few moments later, he hurried out. 'I've phoned for an ambulance. Do you mind if I borrow your pony to get to the crash?' He took over Misty's reins. 'It'll be quicker than saddling one of ours.'

2 *A pony mistrusts us*

When the ambulance arrived, Rob decided to go with his mother to the hospital, leaving Babs and me and Fiona to carry on at the pony farm.

'There's only Macgregor to feed,' Rob told us hurriedly as he climbed into the back of the ambulance. 'The stallion can be a bit tricky – especially with people he doesn't know. He's not really vicious but I'd hate any of you to get kicked. The safest thing would be to fill a hay-net and sling it to him over the door.'

Fiona at once decided that she did not want to go anywhere near the stallion. Although she was a school-friend of Babs, she had never been a truly horsy person. In the past, when I had been staying with my cousin, it had taken us quite a lot of persuasion to coax her to ride Patch.

On the other hand, Babs and I, with our experience of ponies and horses of all kinds–see *Jackie Won a Pony; Ten Ponies and Jackie; Jackie's Pony Patrol; Jackie and the Pony Boys,* etc., etc.,–weren't going to be intimidated by a mere pony stallion!

So, back at the pony farm, we told Fiona to keep right out of the way and to mix Scamp's meat and dog meal and give it to him for his tea; then we filled a hay-net, took a scoopful of pony-nuts and went determinedly to Macgregor's loose-box. True to type, the stallion snorted and blew when he saw us.

'Come on, Macgregor. Good boy.' Babs held out some pony-nuts on the palm of her hand.

The iron-grey ears flicked back, and Macgregor rolled a suspicious eye at Babs and me. Then, realising that all his puffing and snorting wasn't going to scare either of us, he decided that the pony nuts might be worth investigating. Slowly he stretched his head over the half-door to lip them from Babs' hand.

After Macgregor had eaten all the pony-nuts and been shown a lot of fuss, I decided it would be safe enough to go into his box. So, while Babs talked to him, I walked boldly inside, gave him a no-nonsense slap on the quarters and slung the hay-net from its hook. In less than a minute, the stallion was pulling at his hay-net while I stroked his neck and told him firmly that we were going to be friends.

We had just got back to the house when the telephone rang. Fiona was still in the garden with Scamp, so I took the call. Rob was speaking from the hospital.

'How's your mother?' I asked tensely.

'She hasn't come round yet,' said Rob. 'They're X-raying her skull as a precaution, but the doctor feels sure it's just concussion. She'll be out of action for several days at least – and after that she'll have to take things quietly for a week or two ... But that's not really why I rang. Listen carefully, Jackie. One of the mares – Cloud – is due to foal at any time. This will be her first foal and it's important to keep an eye on her to make sure she's all right. She's in the second field beyond the orchard – along by the shore of the loch. Don't fuss her. Just ring back to report how she seems.'

Babs and I, with Fiona, hurried down the length of the garden and through the orchard. As we went through the first field several leggy yearlings jostled towards us. Fiona flinched and drew a little closer to

Babs and me as one of them playfully kicked up his legs, but I had to admire her as she walked steadily on. She seemed to have made up her mind that she was not going to be much use on a pony farm unless she took herself in hand.

We climbed the stile into the second meadow which ran along the shore. This field was more sheltered than the others, particularly at the far end where clumps of gorse and hawthorn enclosed a dip.

As we neared the hollow we saw several pony mares standing in a group. They seemed to be looking at something which lay on the grass. As we drew nearer we saw that it was small and creamy, and one of the mares – a dapple-grey as so many of the Highland ponies seemed to be – was licking it energetically.

'Cloud's foal!' breathed Babs in awe. 'She's had it already. A dear little dun with a black stripe down his back. Isn't he gorgeous?'

As she spoke, I noticed that there was a stallion among the ponies surrounding the mare. I realised, at once, that he should not have been in that field.

As I paused, wondering what to do, the stallion caught our scent. He raised his crested head and gazed across at us. Meanwhile the mares gathered protectively round the foal as it tried to struggle to its uncontrolled legs. Then the stallion snorted and cantered in our direction as if he wanted to drive us away.

'Don't take any notice,' I told Fiona. 'It's probably only a try-on. If we stand our ground he'll swerve away. To run would be disastrous.'

16

'That's all very well,' said Babs, 'but we've got to get him out of this field.'

'Must we?' Fiona tried to keep her voice steady as the stallion came closer. 'He doesn't seem very pleased as it is.'

'Don't flap, Fiona. Just walk quietly to the nearest fence.' Babs moved in front of her friend as the stallion snorted nearer. 'Then run back to the house and 'phone Rob for instructions. Bring a halter back with you if he wants us to try to catch the stallion.'

Babs and I stood firm while Fiona slipped through the fence.

Sure enough, once the stallion had seen that we weren't going to let ourselves be scared, he swerved back to the mares.

We sat on the fence and watched. Cloud's foal had gained his feet and was taking his first feed, his baby tail flicked as his mother nuzzled him encouragingly. The other mares stood in a half-circle, watching like inquisitive aunts, but the stallion was now half-way between the group and us, still looking quite fierce.

I called to him softly: 'It's all right, boy. We're your friends.'

'Yes,' added Babs. 'We don't want to harm your wives or your baby, you silly.'

The stallion ignored our advances. Obviously he wasn't ready to trust us. So we just sat quietly on the fence, trying to get a peep now and then at the foal who was half-hidden behind its mother and the pony 'aunts'.

18

What a perfect scene it was! And what a worthwhile job Mrs Duncan was doing helping to keep alive this grand breed of Highland ponies. How dreadful it would be if she had to give up. It was not only this afternoon's accident which prompted this thought, I recalled something which Fiona had confided to Babs and me while we had all been waiting at the railway station for her aunt to turn up with the horse-box after our journey.

'I'm worried about Aunt Isabel,' Fiona had told us. 'Mummy says she's up to her neck in debt. This summer will decide whether she has to give up the pony farm.'

'But why?' Babs had asked. 'I would have thought there was a good market for Highland ponies. According to the pony magazines, Americans and Australians pay high prices for British animals.'

'So Mummy says,' Fiona had agreed. 'But the trouble is Aunt Isabel has a rival – a Miss Elspeth Gordon who used to run a riding school about fifteen miles away. When she heard that Aunt Isabel seemed to be doing well out of pony breeding she came over to Lochside on a "friendly" visit – just to find out all she could, to spy!'

'The sneaky thing!' Babs hadn't been able to contain her indignation.

'Yes,' agreed Fiona. 'She picked Aunt Isabel's brain, copied her methods, out-bid her for new brood mares and poached her best customers. There just isn't room for the two of them in the same district.'

19

So that was the situation! And, with Rob's mother now out of action, things looked like becoming worse. The immediate future of the Lochside Pony Stud depended very much on Rob, Babs and me, with the willing, but distinctly nervous, help of poor Fiona.

Would we be able to cope?

3　*I fall into a trap*

There was more to Fiona than one might have imagined, however. Going to the farm-house to telephone Rob at the hospital must have given her time to pull herself together because, when she came back to where Babs and I were waiting in the field, she was carrying a bowl of oats as well as the halter.

'I couldn't get through to Rob,' she explained. 'A nurse answered the telephone. She said there wasn't a boy in the hall.'

'That could mean that your aunt has come round and they've fetched Rob to see her in the ward.' I took the bowl from her. 'It was a brainwave of yours, Fiona, to bring the oats.' I nodded towards the stallion who had turned his head towards us and was now sniffing the air interestedly. 'The scent of food seems to have made his nibs a little more pleased to see us.'

The stallion trotted towards us and I managed to get the halter over his head while he sampled the oats. Then, with Babs going ahead and using the rest of the feed as a lure, we took him back to the farm.

Just as we reached the yard, my spaniel Scamp managed to escape from the kitchen where Fiona had put him to finish his tea. Ears flying he raced over the cobbles and darted under the fence to investigate the yearlings in the nearest field.

'Come back, Scamp! You'll get kicked!' Babs and Fiona chased after him while I shut the loose-box door on the stallion.

At that moment the telephone bell shrilled from the house, and I hurried to answer it, thinking it would probably be Rob phoning from the hospital.

I was wrong.

As I picked up the telephone a woman's voice enquired: 'Is that the Lochside Pony Stud?'

'It is. Who's speaking, please?'

'Who's that then?' the woman countered, disregarding my question. 'I don't know your voice.'

'Probably not. I'm Jackie Hope, I'm staying here with my cousin, and Mrs Duncan's niece, Fiona. Can I help you?'

'That's kind of you to offer.' The woman's voice softened. 'But as a matter of fact, I was wondering if I could help *you*. I've just heard about the accident. How dreadful it must have been for you all! What exactly happened?'

I poured out the details explaining how Mrs Duncan was in hospital and likely to be there for some time.

'But how can you possibly manage without her?' said the woman. 'I understand that you have a number of mares about to foal, and then, of course, there'll be the Strathtay Spring Show. Mrs Duncan was entering for that, surely?'

'So Fiona said.' It was a relief to pour out our

worries to such an understanding stranger. 'Her aunt
has several mares entered for the brood-mares class
and two mares and foals in one of the other sections.
One of the stallions was in for the championship, and
then, of course, there'd have been some of the yearlings.'

'What a pity!' The woman paused for a moment.
'How disappointing for those Americans who were
coming specially to see Mrs Duncan's entries at the
show. From Nebraska, weren't they?'

'Not from Nebraska.' I cast my mind back to what
Fiona had told us earlier. 'From New Jersey, I think.'

'Yes, of course. Would it be the Bramwells from
Trenton?'

'No, that wasn't the name. Maitland, I think they're
called.'

'Oh, yes, Maitland.' The woman at the other end of
the line repeated the name, and it wasn't until afterwards that I realised that she must have been writing
it down! 'Well, I must go now.' She was suddenly
brisk. 'I'm so glad we've had this chat. Cheery-bye!'

'Just a minute!' I said before she could ring off. 'Mrs
Duncan will be pleased to know that you telephoned.
Will you give me your name?'

'My name . . .' The woman paused, and suddenly I
had a dreadful feeling as to the reason she might be
hesitant to reveal her identity. 'I'm Elspeth Gordon.'

I could have kicked myself!

What an idiot I had been, giving away all that semi-
secret information. I'd played right into Elspeth Gordon's hands. There was only one thing for it. I'd have

to let Rob know what I'd done right away so that he would be fore-warned.

My mouth was dry as I dialled the number of the hospital call-box.

This time Rob answered the phone. He was so quick that he must have been standing right outside the box. 'What on earth have you all been doing?' he demanded. 'I've been trying to get through for ages, but first there was no reply and then the number was engaged. What's been going on?'

I took a deep breath and confessed how Elspeth Gordon had tricked me to reveal stable-secrets.

For a moment Rob remained silent. Then he seemed to swallow as if he might have been counting up to ten. At last he said fairly calmly: 'It's bad luck, of course, Jackie, but you're not to blame. You wouldn't know what a menace Miss Gordon is. She's a human ferret! Well, thank goodness you had the sense to tell me what happened. I'll get an airmail letter from the WRVS trolley right away and mail it to the Maitlands tonight. I'll put them in the picture about Elspeth Gordon before she tries to get in touch.' I opened my mouth to ask if that was wise but just then he broke off: 'I've got to go now, Jackie. A nurse has beckoned. Perhaps Mum really has come round. She may want to speak to me. So long.'

'Just a minute!' I exclaimed urgently realising that I hadn't yet told him about the birth of Cloud's foal. 'Are you there, Rob?'

But the line was dead. Rob had gone.

That evening, Rob told us that his mother's X-ray results had been satisfactory. There was no real damage to her skull.

'All the same, she's not right,' he went on. 'She keeps coming round and then passing out again. The doctor says she's suffering from severe concussion and may have to stay in hospital for quite a while.'

Almost before he had finished speaking, the telephone rang. The colour drained from his face as he picked up the instrument and we all tensed, thinking that the call might be from the hospital with some untoward news of Mrs Duncan.

The voice at the other end was so clear that we could hear every word.

'Is that you, Rob? This is Elspeth Gordon.'

Rob's face closed. 'Now look here, Miss Gordon, there's no point your telephoning to try to get any

more information. Jackie Hope's already told me how you pumped her about our private business . . .'

'Just listen a minute, Rob,' Elspeth Gordon said firmly. 'I've only phoned to do you a good turn.'

'I wonder!' Rob said bitterly.

'Goodness knows why I should fuss myself when you're being so downright rude.' Miss Gordon now sounded annoyed. 'All the same, I won't let your unmannerly hostility stand in the way when one of your animal's lives might be at stake. About half-an-hour ago, I took a drive in your direction, just to satisfy myself that everything was all right.'

'To have a good nose round, more likely.' Babs' aside was penetrating.

'I'll disregard that interruption,' said Elspeth Gordon. 'The fact is, Rob, I noticed a group of your mares down in the hollow by the river. They seemed to be clustered round something. I looked through my night-glasses to see whether it might be a foal. Actually, though, it was a very distressed mare. Obviously she'd recently foaled, but the foal was missing! It was nowhere in sight, in fact. I was driving back to phone you when I saw a reddish-coloured mare with a very young foal upon the hill above the salmon ladder. The foal was trying to feed, but it was obvious the mare wasn't his mother. You see, she hadn't any milk.'

Her voice became urgent.

'You'd better get out there right away. If that foal's not returned to its mother tonight, it may be dead by morning!'

26

4 Foal in danger

'It sounds as though Pixie may have taken Cloud's foal,' groaned Rob. 'She must have wanted a foal so badly that she couldn't wait another couple of weeks until her own was born.'

'And so she's stolen Cloud's,' said Babs. 'How dreadful!'

'It certainly is.' Rob handed round torches. 'Miss Gordon's quite right for once. It's vital we find Cloud's foal within a few hours.' He glanced towards Scamp who, roused from his basket by all the commotion was now gazing up at us, wagging his tail as though wondering whether all this excitement foretold a walk.

Rob looked thoughtful as he patted him. 'It might not be a bad idea, old chap, for you to come. Put him on his lead, Jackie. He might be able to pick up the scent of the foal.'

If I live to be a hundred I shall never forget that night. There we were, Rob, Fiona, Babs and me, with Scamp padding alongside, setting out to look for Cloud's missing foal.

As we reached the hollow in the second field, I gripped Scamp's collar, trying to make him understand what we wanted him to do.

'Here, Scamp. Seek!' In the light of Babs' torch I indicated the flattened area of grass where Cloud's foal had been born. 'Sniff, Scamp! Yes *seek*!'

To this day I'm not sure whether Scamp really picked up the foal's scent or whether he was on the trail of a rabbit, but he gave a sudden whimper and then streaked off, nose to the ground. In the torchlight we caught glimpses of him busily quartering.

Once I thought I saw the mare and foal in the lee of a big rock. I shone my torch and a black-faced ewe with twin lambs skittered away into the night.

'Oh dear! I've got a stitch.' Fiona clutched her side as we reached the ridge.

'I think we'll stand more chance of finding the mare and foal if we split up,' said Rob. 'Jackie, keep Scamp with you because he knows you best. The rest of us had better search in other directions. If you see Pixie and the foal, just shout.'

'Right!' I panted after my spaniel who was now working his way up the rocky bed of the burn. As I ran, I swung my torch on to every thorn bush or clump of gorse. Snuffing and wooffling, nose still to the ground, Scamp was certainly on some trail and I prayed that it might be that of the foal.

The night was becoming colder. Hill-side and heather were already wet with dew. There was going to be a frost. The need to find the foal became really urgent.

In the bright moonlight I could plainly see Scamp. He was working his way along the burn. Suddenly he

seemed to come on an even stronger scent. Nose up now, he left the bed of the burn and ran, ears flying, towards the edge of the hillside.

'Scamp, be careful!' I shouted.

I caught my breath as my spaniel seemed to plunge over the edge.

'*Scamp!*' I gasped, running after him.

Shining my torch downwards, I was relieved to see that the drop was, after all, not as steep as the moonlight had made it appear. Below me, Scamp was making his way down a zig-zag path to a quarry below. As he sped down to the bottom, I saw something move.

Down there in the moonlight was Pixie and, on the ground beside her, lay Cloud's foal!

'Rob! Babs! Fiona!' I shouted before I hurried down the path after Scamp. 'Pixie and the foal are down in a quarry. Scamp's found them.'

As I neared the bottom, Scamp ran to meet me. He thrust his cold nose into my hand before bounding back to circle Pixie and the foal.

Rob clattered down the path behind me. At the noise the foal raised its head and looked at us, before staggering to its lanky legs.

'Thank goodness!' Rob breathed and, amid a trickle of falling shale, Babs and Fiona scrambled down to join us.

'What on earth are we going to do?' Babs asked, gazing in dismay as the foal's legs collapsed under it. 'That poor little thing's exhausted. He can't possibly walk all the way back to the farm.'

'No,' said Rob, 'but I might manage to carry him a hundred yards to the road that the Land Rovers use when there's a grouse shoot. You girls stay here with Pixie and the foal and I'll go and wake Sandy Macpherson. He's the ghillie at Auch n' Creary. I'll wake him and get him to drive our horse-box up here.'

When Rob had gone Babs, Fiona and I put our anoraks over the foal to keep him warm. He lay trembling slightly and Pixie stood by nuzzling him while Scamp sat nearby, importantly on guard.

It seemed a long time before we heard the horse-box rumble up the track with Rob and Sandy Macpherson.

They let down the ramp and, while Babs coaxed Pixie inside, Sandy Macpherson picked up the foal and laid him gently in the straw. Then we all squashed on to the front seat in the cab and Scamp jumped on to my knee.

When we reached Lochside, Rob led Pixie back to her field and brought Cloud to the horse-box in her place.

The foal raised his head from the straw as Cloud's unshod hooves clopped across the yard. His mother gave a whicker and walked up the ramp into the horse-box while we all held our breath, waiting to see whether she would accept him despite Pixie's intervention.

To our relief her tongue flicked out.

'He'll be all right now.' Rob gave a sigh of satisfaction as the mare licked the foal all over to remove any scent of Pixie from his coat.

Then I felt Scamp's rough tongue touch my hand.

'It's all thanks to you Scamp,' I said, 'that this particular episode has a happy ending.'

'Thanks to Elspeth Gordon, too, I suppose,' Fiona added fairly. 'If she hadn't been snooping round Aunt Isabel's land, we'd never have known that Pixie had stolen Cloud's foal until it was too late. There must be some good in the woman, after all.'

'Not much, I'm sure!' Babs said sceptically.

'Hear! hear!' agreed Rob. 'I expect her main aim in letting us know about the foal was to put us under an obligation to her. She probably thinks that, when she's driven Mum out of business, she'll be able to buy the farm cheaply and have us tamely working for her.' His jaw set. 'No way! Am I glad I sent off that airmail letter to New Jersey, warning the Maitlands to be on their guard against her tricks!'

I looked at him blankly, wondering just what he had written. I had an uneasy feeling that the American pony buyer might not react well to Rob's letter. Not knowing the full facts, might it not appear to them that he was unfairly running down a rival?

If only Rob hadn't been called away from the telephone after voicing his intention of buying an airmail letter from the hospital that afternoon!

Then I might have been able to state my anxiety and perhaps urge him to have second thoughts.

Now it was too late. There would be no point in raising the matter now that he had already posted the letter.

I tried to stifle my misgivings, but they would not go away. However, there was nothing I could do about the dilemma. All that remained was for Babs and I to do our best to help Rob to run the pony farm smoothly and to make sure that the stock was in the best possible condition when the time came for the Maitlands to pay their fateful visit.

Saying nothing, I hopefully crossed my fingers for luck.

5   A scare for Fiona

There was a phone call from the hospital early next morning to say that Mrs Duncan had fully regained consciousness and wanted to see Rob.

'The Sister says it's vital that I go in to visit her right away,' he told us, 'otherwise she may have a set-back.' His gaze travelled from Fiona to Babs and me. 'Do you girls think you can cope with feeding and mucking out the two stallions? You could let Cloud and her foal out of the horse-box and put them in the orchard where Pixie can't interfere again.'

Picking up his jacket, Rob ran across the yard and down the lane to the village to catch the bus. Then Babs, Fiona and I crossed to the horse-box and let down the ramp. Cloud and her foal turned contented heads towards us. They were happy together, mother and baby son. We felt very tender towards them as we led them to the orchard.

'I wonder what name Rob will give him,' I mused as the foal kicked up his heels and cantered beneath the white canopy of pear and damson blossom.

'Laird of Lochside,' Fiona said with a smile. 'Rob's already decided. His sire, the dun stallion, is Highland Laird so there has to be 'Laird' in the name to carry on the family tree.'

We were gazing so fondly at the pony mother and her foal that we had quite forgotten about Misty and Patch who were in the small paddock adjacent to the orchard. Forgotten, that is, until we heard the noise of breaking branches and turned to see Babs' mischievous skewbald trying to pull down the hedge to reach the orchard. Just as the other ponies had been inquisitive the previous day, Patch was now eager to inspect the foal.

'Patch, you bad pony!' As Babs ran to cope, she called back over her shoulder to Fiona and me: 'You two start mucking out. I won't be long.'

I thought Fiona seemed unusually quiet as we walked towards the loose-boxes and I supposed that she was feeling scared at the prospect of having to come to close quarters with the stallions.

'I'll deal with Macgregor,' I said, remembering that the older and bigger of the two animals could be tricky. 'You take some hay to Highland Laird. You made friends with him yesterday when we got him from the field. He'll know you now, so it shouldn't be any problem.'

Without thinking any more about it, I went in to Macgregor, tipped some hay into his rack and tied him up to pull at it while I removed the soiled bedding. I was about to wheel away the dirty straw when I noticed that Fiona was standing in the middle of the yard looking unhappy.

'Have you given Highland Laird his fresh water?' I asked.

She shook her head. 'I haven't taken in the hay either,' she confessed. 'I did try, honestly. But I was just about to go in when he turned his head and gave me a look.'

'A *look*?' I repeated puzzled. 'What kind of look?'

'A really bad-tempered one.' Fiona shuddered.

'Oh, that!' I said lightly. 'It's just a trick – a game.'

I took Fiona's arm and led her towards Highland Laird's loose-box. 'You and I will cope together.'

'Must we?' Fiona sighed.

'Yes,' I said firmly. 'You simply can't go on being scared when there's really no reason.'

I opened the loose-box door. Fiona stood just inside watching me as I took in Highland Laird's hay.

The stallion rolled his eyes.

'You do like to pretend to be fierce, don't you?' I said. 'But really you're just the same as any other pony, and you do like a fuss.'

I patted him as he pulled at the hay. 'You see, Fiona,' I said triumphantly. 'All done by love.'

'You're right, Jackie.' Fiona came into the loose-box with me. 'Stand out of the way and let me fuss him.'

I watched as Fiona cautiously patted Highland Laird. Munching, the stallion turned his head to have his nose stroked. Fiona obliged.

'Now we'll always be friends,' she told him and, over her shoulder, she said to me: 'I'm glad you didn't let me funk it.'

Suddenly, without warning, a mouse that had been hiding in the straw, growing more and more frightened by our voices and the stallion's munching, decided to bolt, scuttling right between Highland Laird's feet.

Unfortunately, Highland Laird was terrified of mice. With a startled whinny, he shied, knocking down Fiona. Then he reared.

I made a grab for his head collar, but couldn't reach it. He came crashing down, his fore-feet landing a few inches from Fiona's face as she lay on the floor too frightened to move. Then he reared again.

'Cover your head with your hands and roll clear!' I shouted to Fiona in alarm.

I managed to grab Highland Laird's head-collar as he came down and dragged him away as Fiona shakily crawled to the door.

What an idiot I've been, I thought, as she picked herself up and ran to the house, coaxing Fiona into handling the horse before she was ready. Now it would be harder than ever for Fiona to keep her nerve and be happy and at ease with the many different ponies on the farm.

Another scare and she might be put off horses for life!

6 *Mystery stallion*

Next day I decided it would be best to keep Fiona well away from the two stallions.

'Be an angel and groom Misty and Patch,' I said, knowing that she was used to Babs' pony and mine. 'Babs and I will help Rob to see to the others.'

After we had completed the mucking out and grooming, we helped Rob to school the mares in the practice ring in readiness for the Strathtay Show. When it came to the turn of Cloud and her foal, he chose Fiona to accustom the little Laird of Lochside to being handled. I was glad to see that she was at her ease with such a small creature. Fiona made much of him and patted him while Babs held Cloud who watched anxiously. The mother thrust her nose forward and whickered as Fiona slipped a small head-collar over the foal's muzzle, smoothed the head-band behind his ears and buckled the throat-lash.

To our relief Laird of Lochside, though puzzled, was docile, letting himself be led round the ring by Fiona while Babs accompanied with his mother.

We spent most of the morning training the show stock. Then, after soup, a cheese roll and a tomato, we decided to go for a ride. Rob rode Macgregor, Babs rode Patch. I rode Misty and we mounted Fiona on Highland Lassie, a cream-coloured Western Isles pony who seemed quiet and willing.

Stumpy tail awag, Scamp ran eagerly ahead as we clip-clopped down the lane behind him. He halted at the fork to see which way we would go. When we chose the stony track leading into the hills, he bounded ahead, nose to the ground to sniff any exciting scents.

Misty, too, was enjoying herself. She broke into a canter as soon as we left the track for the soft turf of the hill-side. A stonechat flew from a bramble bush and Patch shied from sheer high spirits, nearly unseating Babs.

'This is super!' Fiona felt happy on Highland Lassie but soon Rob, Babs and I left her behind. Although Highland Lassie was a fine pony, she had been bred for stalking and her stocky build did not give her the speed of the others.

Suddenly I caught sight of a group of Highland ponies, mostly greys, showing up against a hill-top rock. They belonged to the Lochside Stud. How wonderful they were and what a great life Mrs Duncan and Rob had at the pony farm with them! 'Look, Jackie!' Babs' excited voice called across to me as she and Patch cantered level. 'Over there!' I followed her gaze to see a big bay stallion gallop from the far side of the herd with Rob and Macgregor hard after him.

'A strange stallion and obviously one who shouldn't be with the Lochside herd.' I clapped my heels to Misty's sides and wheeled her to head him off. 'Come on Babs. Let's help Rob round him up.'

Ahead of us ran Scamp, ears flapping, as he streaked towards Rob and the now bolting stranger.

'Call your dog back, Jackie!' Rob yelled to me when Scamp made straight for the horse.

Breathlessly I tried to whistle, but Scamp was deaf to all calls. He put on an extra burst of speed to reach the stallion as he neared the stone wall that ran up the mountain-side.

The stallion rose to the wall and, as Misty and I plunged into a hollow, taking a short cut to try to head the stallion back, a sheep struggled to her feet on the far side. The stallion also saw the sheep. He hesitated, twisted in mid-air and then slipped into a gully which lay between the wall and a sheep-fold on the other side. All I could see of him now was his head and threshing fore-feet. As Babs and I galloped nearer he was thrusting out his fore-legs, frantic to escape from the gully.

Handing my reins to Babs, I dismounted and ran to catch Scamp who was standing on the edge of the gully, looking down at the stallion and barking excitedly. Meanwhile Rob was in the gully with the unfortunate stallion.

Somehow Rob managed to get the spare halter, which he always carried, over the stallion's head and, as I hurried to help, I heard him say: 'Yes, now that you've landed yourself in this mess, you're quite glad to be caught! Come on!' He tried to steady the struggling animal. 'We must get you out of here! But how?'

7   Threat to the pony farm

I ran along the top of the gully as Rob tried to persuade the stallion to follow him along the bottom of the ditch. Their way was barred by a roll of barbed wire.

'Don't tear yourself, Jackie. But try to pull that wire

out of the way,' Rob called quickly. 'If I can get him past that, we should be on firmer ground.'

As I plunged into the mud at the bottom of the gully, dirty water squelched over my shoes. The legs of my jeans were soaking. Trying to avoid the barbs, I tugged at the heavy roll of wire.

'Hang on, Jackie!' Fiona's voice came from the top of the gully. 'Highland Lassie and I have just got here. I'm unbuckling her reins. See if you can pass them through the roll of barbed wire. Perhaps, between us, we can manage to haul it clear.'

As we hauled up the roll, the bay stallion made a bid

for freedom, kicking up his heels and trying .o jerk away from Rob who was equally determined to hang on. Keeping a grip on the halter rope, he walked forward calmly.

'There, boy! That's the end of the gully.' He clambered out and tugged at the rope to help the horse on to firmer ground.

With a scrabble of hooves the stallion heaved himself out. Then, to our surprise, he stood quietly while Rob ran a gentle hand down his forelegs. 'So you're quite used to being handled,' Rob mused as he felt for any injury, 'and you're obviously pure Arab. Somewhere you've got an owner who'll be glad to see you again.'

Back at Lochside, the Arab stallion made a fuss about going into a strange loose-box and Rob had to entice him with oats. He rolled his eyes, giving me an unsure look, when, helped by Babs, I took water and hay to him.

We were careful to shut both halves of the door in case he tried to jump out, with the risk of stunning himself. Then Rob hurried indoors to telephone the police and report his find.

After tea Rob took the bus into town to visit his mother at the hospital. When he came back he seemed worried, so much so that he had to tell us three girls what was on his mind.

'It seems Mum isn't making the progress she should,' he said as he sipped hot chocolate and nibbled a biscuit. 'The Sister says her temperature keeps going up and down and they can't find out why. They're doing all sorts of tests.'

'Poor Aunt Isabel!' sighed Fiona.

'Perhaps she's worrying about what's happening here,' I said.

'More than likely,' Rob agreed unhappily. 'Of course, it hasn't helped to have Elspeth Gordon telephoning her, offering to buy us out for peanuts because she's anxious that, without some "responsible" adult in charge, we may lose this year's foals and every penny we've saved.'

'Miss Gordon telephoned and said that!' Babs' eyes flashed.

'Too true she did,' Rob said grimly. 'Mum tried to make a joke of it when she told me, but I could see it had made her really worried. I know she wouldn't have said anything about it if it hadn't been very much on her mind.'

'Then there's only one thing for it, Rob,' Babs said determinedly. 'When you go in to the hospital tomorrow, you'll just have to let us all go in with you. We can see her two at a time and tell her exactly how things are.'

'Good idea, Babs,' Fiona agreed. 'When Aunt Isabel hears from all of us how well we're doing maybe she'll relax, stop worrying, and start getting better.'

Next day hospital visiting was in the afternoon and, when we went into the ward, we were surprised to find Mrs Duncan sitting up in bed wearing her best bed-jacket. She had put on some lipstick, rubbed 'blusher' into her cheeks and was determinedly trying to be bright and cheerful. But somehow, the more cheerful she pretended to be, the more worried we all felt because her gaiety was so obviously forced.

'Tell me just what you've been doing,' she said when Babs and I replaced Rob and Fiona at her bedside. 'Don't keep anything back. How are the foals? And what about the Strathtay Show? You must remind Rob to rehearse the mares and foals thoroughly. And, of course, Macgregor must enter for the stallion championship.'

Babs and I looked at each other. We were both wondering whether Macgregor would be in the show at all. Somehow, that morning, he had injured his foreleg. It was a nasty gash and Rob had summoned the vet to put in stitches. It might not be better in time for the show, and, even when it did heal, it would leave a scar.

'Don't worry, Mrs Duncan,' Babs said with forced brightness. 'Everything's under control. Rob's rehearsed the entries and we've all helped. Lochside Stud will do as well in the show as if you were there yourself to take charge.'

That did it. Mrs Duncan sat bolt upright, plucking at the bed-clothes.

'But I shall be at the show!' Her voice rose in agitation. 'You three girls and Rob can't show the ponies by yourselves. Anyway, Fiona's too nervous. And there are those American pony-buyers – the Maitlands

— coming. I'm counting on selling them at least a couple of mares and some yearlings. If I don't, the pony farm's finished. Of course, I'll be at the Strathtay Show!'

8 Challenge from a rival

For the next few days we worked harder than ever to make sure that everything went smoothly at Lochside.

Things never do go right at pony farms for long, however, and the next setback was that Macgregor's leg became infected and the vet had to give him an injection. Then we had to apply hot fomentations every four hours.

Meanwhile Lochside Gypsy started to foal. She was a young mare and this was her first foal. Again Rob had to summon the vet and he and Mr Urquhart were up half the night until at last the foal – a filly – arrived.

At the same time we were having trouble with the mystery stallion. He kicked at the door of his loose-box, rolling his eyes and laying flat his ears when anybody took in water or food. He even snapped at Rob.

'I'll be glad when he's claimed,' Rob said exasperatedly after the bay had lashed out and sent the feed bucket spinning from his hands. 'Keeping him in is making him feel hard done by, and we can't risk turning him out.'

He telephoned the police. The local sergeant told him that he had no news about the stallion. They had contacted other police stations over a wide area but nobody had reported a stallion missing.

'It gets more and more mystifying,' Rob said as he set off with three of the ponies to the forge. 'A valuable Arab stallion! You'd have thought his owners would have raised a hue and cry. If he were mine, I'd be combing the countryside until I found him.'

Babs sighed. 'We'll just have to put up with him until the police do find his owner.'

After Rob had gone, Babs and I saddled Misty and Patch. Fiona had decided against riding that morning. She wanted to stay with Cloud and Laird of Lochside to accustom the foal to being handled in time for the show.

As we trotted down the lane, Babs and I saw the postman toiling up from the village. I called to Scamp to stop him jumping at the bicycle. My spaniel had made friends with our postman at home, and now he tended to look on anyone anywhere with a mail satchel as his special pal.

The postman lingered to talk. 'You're the young ladies who are staying at Lochside, aren't you? How's Mrs Duncan? Not home yet?'

'No. She'll be in hospital for another week or two.' I explained about Rob's mother's set-back.

'Pity! But perhaps this will cheer her up.' The postman showed us an airmail letter. 'It seems to be from the States. Let's hope it's from one of those rich American buyers young Rob was telling me about.'

Babs stretched out her hand for the letter. 'We'll

save you pushing your bike up the hill. Rob's out at the moment but we'll give him the letter as soon as he gets back.'

We continued our ride, turning on to a grassy track that led up a valley between the hills. Primroses starred the burnside and a blackbird was trilling his spring song from one of the thorn bushes. Hopefully, we felt that things were sure to be better for Rob and his mother from now on.

How wrong we were!

The first hint of trouble came as we crossed the stream over the plank bridge further up the valley and glimpsed a long bonneted red sports car nosing its way down towards Lochside.

I tensed, reining up Misty. 'That's Elspeth Gordon's car, Babs. I've seen it before. I'd know it anywhere.'

'You're right.' Babs turned Patch towards the pony farm. 'Come on. She must be going to Lochside. The road doesn't lead anywhere else.'

'That's true.' I touched Misty with my heels. 'We can't leave Fiona to cope on her own. Let's rout the rival!'

With Scamp streaking ahead, Babs and I neck-reined our ponies down the twisting path to crash Misty and Patch through last year's bracken at top speed. Miss Gordon had left her car behind the larches and was hurrying towards the Lochside stable yard.

As we neared the pony farm we heard her shout:

'Put that broom down, girl! And, for heaven's sake, keep calm!'

Fiona must be in trouble. My heart sank as I heard a stallion's neigh, followed by the whinny of a startled mare. Oh dear!

'Come on, Misty. Faster!'

A couple of lengths ahead of Babs and Patch, I rounded the turn of the drive and saw that our mystery stallion was dangerously at large. He was threatening Fiona!

Elspeth Gordon was running towards him. Meanwhile Babs's school-friend was frenziedly brandishing the stable broom while, in a corner of the yard, the Highland mare, Cloud, stood protectively in front of her foal. Somehow the stallion had managed to push up the latch of his loose-box door. Fiona must have been leading the mare and foal round the yard when the stallion escaped. Fiona must have thought he was going to attack Cloud and the foal. So she had tried to drive him off with the stable broom. The stallion had felt himself threatened, and now was in a really ugly mood.

As Babs and I tied our ponies and Scamp to the railings Fiona, in utter panic, waved the broom in the bay stallion's face.

'Stop, Fiona,' Babs yelled. 'Put it down!'

Miss Gordon moved in from another angle. The stallion swerved to dodge her, and knocked Fiona down, before breaking into a wild canter round the yard.

At that moment, Elspeth Gordon saw Babs and me. She glanced at Fiona and noticed that she had somehow managed to scramble to her feet. Then, deliberately folding her arms, Elspeth turned with a challenging look to Babs and me.

'Go on, then. Let's see how you two so-called pony girls can cope.'

9 Rob's letter misfires

For a moment we were nonplussed. Babs opened her mouth to shout at Elspeth Gordon, but I silenced her.

'That won't help. Stay where you are, Babs, please. Keep talking to Fiona. Try to calm her. I've got an idea.'

Remembering that the stallion like most horses, enjoyed a dry crust, I dashed to the kitchen, grabbed one from the bread tin and held it out to him as he circled the yard. He turned his head to look at me; then he pulled up, trembling. Nervously he came forward to collect the offering. As he took it, I was able to get a grip on his halter. I led him back to the loose-box, shut him in and wedged the latch with a piece of wood.

'That'll keep you safe,' I said as he turned to pull at his hay. 'Oh, yes, I know you're bored by being kept in and I hope, for your sake as well as ours, that we're soon able to trace your owner.'

As I stopped speaking I heard Miss Gordon scolding Fiona. 'That animal will never trust you again, you silly girl! Why did you lose your nerve? You ought never to be allowed within miles of any horse.'

'What business is it of yours?' demanded Babs as I

went across to join her in Fiona's defence. 'Everybody can't have nerves of iron like you.'

'Really! How rude!' Elspeth Gordon said coolly. 'And what a muddle you're making of things! The sooner Mrs Duncan realises what's going on and decides to accept my offer to take over this place, the better it will be for the ponies. Why, you haven't even bothered to see that your boundaries are properly made up. As I was driving here this morning I saw two places where a pony might get out.' She broke off to glance around impatiently. 'Anyway, where's Rob?'

'He's not back yet.' I tried hard to be polite. 'May we give him a message?'

'Yes, tell him to remind his mother that my offer still holds.' Elspeth Gordon produced an air-letter from

her pocket and flaunted it before our eyes. 'I received this today from the Maitlands in New Jersey. They'll be flying over any day now, but it seems it's my ponies they'll be buying after all, not Lochside's.'

'I don't believe it,' flashed Babs. 'They're coming to the UK specially to see Mrs Duncan's ponies.'

'*Were* coming to see Mrs Duncan's ponies,' Elspeth Gordon corrected. 'Things change, you know.' She gave me a meaningful glance. 'After your friend here was kind enough to give me their name, I wrote to the Maitlands via the American Pony Breeders' Club. It seems that Rob had some communication with them, too. Goodness knows what he wrote, but it didn't seem to have pleased them much. It merely made them decide it was my ponies they wanted to inspect with a view to buying.'

She got back into her car and, as she drove away, Fiona burst into tears. 'That woman's beastly – horrible! But what's worse, she's right – about me, I mean. I shouldn't be allowed near ponies or horses. I'm too nervous.'

'Nonsense, Fiona.' I put an arm round her. 'You've come on marvellously. You've been doing very well.'

'Until this happened.' A tear rolled down Fiona's cheek. 'At heart I know I'll always be nervous with ponies. And that's dangerous on a pony farm. It would be better if I went home tomorrow and left you two to help Rob. You're real pony girls.'

'Oh, dry up, and stop feeling sorry for yourself, Fiona!' Babs was exasperated. 'If you think you're no good at ponies, at least you can make yourself useful in the house. Come indoors and help me get the lunch.'

'Yes, Rob's going to need something to pull him round when we show him this.' Forebodingly I gazed at the airmail letter which the postman had given us. 'I wonder what's in it? After what Elspeth Gordon said I can't help feeling it's bad news!'

'We are sorry to hear about your mother's accident,' Rob's face tensed as he read out the contents of the letter on his return, 'and we are even more unhappy about the rest of your letter. It doesn't seem fair to run down a fellow-breeder, as you have done. We must emphasise that our presence at the Strathtay Show does not mean your ponies are the only ones in which we will be interested. We did not know of Miss Elspeth Gordon's stud when we contacted you. Naturally we want to see what she can offer. Please don't build too much on making a sale to us.'

'So that's that!' Rob crumpled the letter. 'Goodness knows where we go from here. I suppose I was an idiot to lay it on so strongly in my letter. But I did feel the Maitlands ought to be warned about Elspeth Gordon's wiles.'

'You weren't to blame,' I said loyally.

Babs nodded. 'Jackie and I ought to have urged you to write another letter to the Maitlands explaining that you'd sent the first airmail in the heat of the moment while you were worried out of your mind over your mother's accident.'

'It's too late now.' Fiona's tone was flat. Tears were trembling on her eyelashes, and she looked utterly defeated. 'Everything's against us! And I've been no help. Elspeth Gordon made me realise that. I'm a disaster where ponies are concerned.'

'Now, Fiona . . .'

'Oh, yes, I am!' She caught at her cousin's sleeve. 'Babs and Jackie have been able to be really helpful. But not me! And so much depends on it. Your future, Rob; and Aunt Isabel's, and all I've been able to do is to make matters worse.' With a sob she broke away from us and set off towards the house, murmuring: 'I'll get the tea.'

Babs moved to follow, but Rob held her back.

'Let her be,' he said wisely. 'I know my cousin Fiona. There's no joy in trying to cheer her up when she gets one of her blue moods. She doesn't want to know. Better let her work off her guilt by doing something useful. Being able to set a good meal on the table and seeing us three tuck in hungrily will soon make her feel better!'

10 Fiona flees

Even so, for the next few days Fiona was subdued and we knew that she was still brooding over having lost her nerve.

Just the same, she didn't seem able to keep away from the mystery stallion's loose-box.

Then at last she told us what was troubling her. We had just finished the mucking out and grooming and Babs took her arm to go in for elevenses.

'Just a minute.' Fiona pulled back. 'The Arab stallion's behaving oddly. He keeps tossing his head. I only hope I didn't hurt him with that broom. I caught him quite a crack when he went for me the other day.'

Babs and I looked across to the Arab's loose-box. Inside, the stallion was arching his neck and jerking his head.

'I suppose something could be irritating him,' I said, moving forward to find out.

Babs put a hand on my arm. 'Hold on a minute, Jackie. Just keep quiet . . . Now listen! Can you hear Rob's transistor in the tack room? I think the stallion's nodding his head in time to the music.' She paused. 'Be an angel and fetch me that lungeing whip that Mrs Duncan keeps by the back door.' She turned to Fiona.

'You go with Jackie and stay out of harm's way. You can watch from the kitchen window.'

Fiona hesitated. 'What are you going to do?'

'Wait and see,' Babs said guardedly. 'Buck up, Jackie. Give me the whip. That's it ... Now stand against the wall.'

She opened the loose-box door. 'Allez-oop!' she called, and moved into the middle of the yard while the bay stallion pranced out with a proud toss of his head.

I watched amazed as, lungeing whip outstretched, Babs kept pace with the circling stallion.

'So that's it!' Rob came out of the tack-room to join us. 'Well done, Babs! You've solved the mystery. The

stallion is a liberty horse from a circus! Knowing that should make it easier to find his owner. Put him back in his loose-box and I'll phone the police. They'll soon locate any circus that has reported a missing Arab.'

Next morning, when Babs and I were grooming Patch and Misty we were surprised to hear a man's voice saying: 'Moonlight. Hey, Moonlight!'

Dandy brush in hand, I turned to see a young policeman gazing at the mystery stallion.

'Moonlight?' queried Babs. 'Is that his name?'

'Aye, and he seems to know it too.' The young policeman shut the door of the Panda car and crossed the yard to examine the stallion. 'It's him all right. He fits the description. He belongs to Fossley's Circus.' He turned to Babs. 'Is young Mr Duncan around? The sergeant told me to ask if he'd be prepared to keep the stallion until the circus returns to this district next week.'

'Rob's not here just now,' Fiona told him. 'But I'm sure he'd agree.'

'Och, then you've got a few more days grace, laddie.' The policeman rubbed the Arab between the eyes. 'You're a sight better off here than you'll be with that circus.' He looked from me to Babs. 'Fossley hasn't got a good name, I'm afraid, where animals are concerned. He's had a couple of prosecutions already.'

'Then does Moonlight have to go back?' Fiona looked serious.

''Fraid so, miss. Mr Fossley's his legal owner, you ken.'

'Then I wish I hadn't noticed Moonlight keeping time with the music!' Fiona gave a heavy sigh. 'I'm a jinx. That's what I am. Unlucky for horses!'

'Don't talk rot, Fiona.' Babs spoke sharply to shake her out of her self-reproach. 'You're becoming a real wet blanket. Now come and show us what you can do. You've learnt to handle Cloud and the foal. So let's see you bring up Cobweb. You can catch her and give her a lesson in being led in hand.'

Fiona took a sieveful of oats and crossed to the field. There were some other young mares with Cobweb and, as Fiona shut the gate, they cantered up, hoping to share the oats. Fiona flinched and I felt sorry for her. If anyone was nervous with ponies, it could be quite frightening to have four young mares jostling and shoving.

Even so, Fiona stood her ground. She gave each of the mares a handful of oats and then held out the sieve to Cobweb.

'Well done!' Babs called encouragingly. 'Now catch her.'

Cautiously, Fiona lifted the bridle to Cobweb's head. The mare was too busy questing the oats to open her mouth for the bit so Fiona hesitated over slipping it in. She muffed it and ended up with the head-piece over Cobweb's ears while the bit was still somewhere beneath the pony's chin.

Startled, Cobweb vigorously shook her head. Fiona jumped out of the way, tugging the reins and the bit banged against Cobweb's muzzle.

The mare reared, squealed and cantered off round the field. Next moment she put her feet through the reins. The leather snapped.

At that moment, Rob came back from the village. He hurried into the field, caught Cobweb, put on her bridle properly and knotted the broken reins.

'Bad luck, Fiona,' he said briefly to his cousin who looked abashed. 'There's no need for you to bother with the ponies, you know. Babs, Jackie and I can cope. Why not take Scamp for a walk?'

'Good idea, Fiona,' I said quickly seeing Babs' school-friend's lip tremble. 'Scamp hasn't had a proper run for ages. You'll be doing him a really good turn.'

Babs and I were too busy for the rest of the morning to bother much about Fiona. We saw her start off with Scamp and then we were fully occupied taking a bunch of unshod mares to the smithy. When we got back to Lochside we expected to find Fiona busy in the kitchen preparing lunch, but there was no sign of her, nor of Scamp.

'Fiona!' Babs called. 'Where are you?'

The only answer was barking from the tack-room into which Fiona had apparently shut Scamp.

As I went into the tack-room to let him out, my gaze fell on an envelope propped on the bench.

'Dear Rob, Babs and Jackie,' Fiona had written.

'I'm going home!

'Don't try to stop me. I'm no use here. Babs and Jackie have been very kind, trying to get me more used to ponies. But that's taking up time when they could be doing other things. There's so much for you all to do, getting ready for the show that I don't want to be a hindrance.

'So I'm off!

'I've packed my case. I shall catch a 'bus into the town and board the afternoon train to Glasgow. From there I can take an Inter-City home.

'I'll ring you tomorrow. Give my love to your Mum, Rob, and try all of you to understand.

                                            Fiona'

As I read the letter aloud Rob entered the tack room.

'The idiot!' he groaned. 'Doesn't Fiona realise that this will worry Mum more than anything?' He looked from Babs to me in despair before turning to the door. 'There's only one thing for it, of course. We've got to get Fiona back!'

11 A desperate ride

Before Rob was even out of the door, a car horn sounded in the lane. A moment later a taxi turned into the yard. In it, pale and shaky-looking, but fully dressed and quite alert, sat Mrs Duncan!

'Great Heavens! Mum!' Rob's jaw dropped. 'What on earth's she doing here? The Sister said last night that she needed at least another week in hospital.'

'She must have discharged herself,' said Babs.

'Only to arrive home in time to hear that Fiona's run away.' I sighed.

'Then there's no need for her to know,' Babs decided quickly. 'Rob, you stay here and welcome your mother. Jackie and I will ride to the station. We must stop Fiona catching the train.'

By road it would have been ten miles to the town, so Babs and I rode cross-country, taking the shortest route over the hills, jumping streams, walls, fences.

Misty and Patch loved the ride. It was almost as good as a drag-hunt to them. Hooves drumming, manes and tails streaming, necks and flanks a-lather, our ponies responded keenly.

As we came within sight of the grey Scottish town,

the clock below the kirk steeple was striking two. The Glasgow train left at half-past. With time in hand, we gave our ponies a breather before trotting through busy streets to the station.

'Now to persuade Fiona to come back.' Babs dismounted and handed Patch's reins to me. 'Wait here, Jackie. I'll talk to her because I know her best.'

'What are you going to say?' I asked.

Babs gave me a purposeful look. 'I shall tell her she must come back, of course. Somebody must look after her aunt, and you and Rob and I are going to be far too busy preparing for the show. I shall simply tell Fiona that her aunt needs nursing and it's up to her to put our school Red Cross lessons into practice.'

Babs was a long time and I thought she couldn't be finding it as easy to persuade Fiona as she'd expected. While I was waiting I loosened Misty's and Patch's girths, rubbed them both down as best I could with my handkerchief, and then walked them round the station fore-court.

We were on our fifth trek when a long-distance express pulled in. I realised with relief that it was not the train to Glasgow for which Fiona was waiting; it had come from that city. Even before the stream of disembarking passengers began to trickle through the ticket-barrier, the train pulled out again, heading north – probably en-route for Inverness.

Among the sprinkling of tweed-suited men and warmly fur-coated women were two passengers who, by the way they were dressed, stood out from the rest.

Noticing the man's stetson hat and cigar and the woman's bright coloured jacket and hat with scarlet leather boots to match, something prickled in my scalp. Even before I saw the trans-Atlantic labels on their luggage, I realised that they were from the USA. Could they be the Maitlands?

I walked Misty and Patch nearer. As I did so, I noticed some heavily embossed initials on the side of the scarlet crocodile leather beauty-box the woman was carrying: C.M. Could that last letter stand for Maitland?

'Excuse me,' I said, hurrying before the man had time to catch the waiting taxi-driver's eye. 'Am I right in thinking that you may be pony people, too? If so, welcome to Scotland!'

'That's real sweet of you, honey.' Mrs Maitland's scarlet lips broke into a smile. 'Hear that, Herman? This young lady's welcoming us to her country.'

Her husband gave me a brief glance before signalling to the taxi. 'Her accent doesn't sound very Scottish to me.' Having assured himself that the taxi was on its way, he turned to eye me shrewdly. 'What do you want, young lady? Has Miss Elspeth Gordon sent you to meet us? And are those two of her ponies . . . ? Nice animals, no doubt, but not what we're looking for.'

'Misty and Patch are not for sale,' I said quickly. 'And I'm certainly not here on behalf of Miss Gordon. I'm helping at Lochside Stud. I believe you're Mr and Mrs Maitland, and I'm glad to have the chance to

speak to you because I want to set the record straight.'

The man's brow creased and he signalled the taxi-driver to put the cases in the boot. 'You're wasting your time, young lady. I'll tell you now that I won't hear a word against Miss Gordon. I've read enough on those lines from Mrs Duncan's son in a disgraceful letter that he wrote to me. Blackening a rival's reputation is a mean trick.'

'Hey! Wait a minute, Herman,' Mrs Maitland protested. 'Don't be so unfriendly.' She gave me a quick smile. 'This young lady has been courteous enough to welcome us. She says she wants to explain. At least give her a hearing.'

'Oh, please listen,' I begged. Herman Maitland hesitated. 'Rob wasn't being malicious. When he wrote that letter to you, he was almost beside himself with worry.'

'Of course.' Mrs Maitland laid a sympathetic hand on my sleeve. 'It must have been terrible for the poor boy, his mother having such a serious accident.'

'Naturally I was sorry to hear about Mrs Duncan's mishap,' Mr Maitland admitted with a sigh. 'It was her son's running down Miss Gordon that made me angry.'

'But you don't know all the facts, Mr Maitland,' I said desperately. 'Granted Rob shouldn't have written that letter: but Miss Gordon really was trying to take an unfair advantage of his mother being out of action.'

I broke off, aware that I might be making matters worse, but Mrs Maitland encouraged me to complete my explanation.

'Go on, sweetie!' she urged. 'Tell just what happened. I know a nice, honest girl like you wouldn't want to mislead us.'

'Well, it was really all my fault,' I explained. 'I'd only just arrived at Lochside and I didn't know what rivals the two pony farms were. So when Miss Gordon rang up and pretended to be sympathetic about Rob's mother's accident, but, at the same time, tried to find out all about you and Mr Maitland as prospective buyers, I fell right into her trap. I told her everything – your name and all about you coming from New Jersey. I just about ruined the best chance Rob and his mother will ever have to make a good sale, and be able to keep Lochside Stud going.' I faced Mr Maitland earnestly. 'If they can't make this sale to you, Rob and his mother will be out of business and Miss Gordon will buy up their farm and ponies for a song. Rob's and his mother's ponies are good. Even better than Miss Gordon's. Really they are.'

I must have sounded at the end of my tether because Mrs Maitland clasped my hands warmly before facing her husband.

'That has the ring of truth to me, Herman. I can understand how worried young Rob Duncan must have been. He'd have been beside himself when he wrote you that letter. Why don't we just go along to Lochside as we'd arranged?'

'No, Cora.' Mr Maitland's jaw was set. 'If there's one thing I've learned in business, it's not to let sentiment interfere with my decisions.'

'But, Herman . . .' Cora began to reason.

Herman faced me unrelentingly.

'That's why, young lady, I've no intention of going near Mrs Duncan's pony farm at this stage. At the same time I shan't visit Miss Elspeth Gordon either.'

'Well, that's something,' conceded his wife.

The American's expression softened slightly.

'I pride myself on being a fair man. So, Jackie, you can tell young Rob Duncan that I shall be attending the show. Tell him to put in his entries. Then I can decide between the Duncan ponies and Miss Gordon's strictly on the results. That way I'll have the judgment of British pony experts to help me make up my mind.'

'Well, that's better.' Cora Maitland gave me a comforting smile. 'At least he hasn't pre-judged the matter. He hasn't made any snap decision to buy Miss Gordon's ponies, honey.'

'I suppose you could say that, Cora,' Mr. Maitland acknowledged gruffly before helping his wife into the taxi. 'We'll await the results of the show. Okay?'

So there was still a glimmer of hope!

If nothing went wrong on the day, the Lochside ponies might still carry off the trophies and then Mr Maitland would buy Mrs Duncan's stock. It was up to Babs, Rob and me to make sure that the Lochside entries did well.

There was still a few more days to make sure that the ponies reached the peak of their form.

12 Encounter with a baddie

A chastened Fiona returned with Babs and me to Lochside Pony Farm. Even so it seemed that our troubles were far from over.

The excitement of coming out of hospital had been too much for Mrs Duncan and she decided to spend the next morning in bed.

I'd just gone up for her breakfast tray when I heard Scamp barking loudly in the yard below. At the same time Mrs Duncan called to me from her bedroom. As I ran into the bedroom, I saw her leaning out of bed trying to crane through the window.

'Something's going on and I can't see what!' she told me, frustratedly. 'Be an angel, Jackie. Look out and report.'

Scamp was still barking wildly and as I peered from the window I saw what looked like an outside horse-box trying to negotiate the turn into the stable yard.

It wasn't like any horse-box that I'd ever seen.

It was painted in red and white stripes!

As I turned to Mrs Duncan to report, Scamp's barking changed to an angry growl. Where were Rob, Babs and Fiona, I wondered? Then I realised that they were probably down in the meadow admiring a new

foal which had been born during the night.

I'll see what's going on,' I told Mrs Duncan. Then, as more growling came from the yard, I called: 'All right, Scamp. I'm coming,' adding, 'Don't stir from that bed, Mrs Duncan.'

As I sped out of the front door I heard what sounded like the crack of a whip, followed by a man's rough voice: 'Bite me, would you? Well, I've handled fiercer animals than you. I'll teach you.'

Someone was threatening Scamp!

I was so angry that I hardly took in the lettering on the side of the horse-box: CARL FOSSLEY'S CIRCUS.

I rushed round the vehicle in time to hear a yelp from Scamp and the same horrid voice: 'Down! Get back! Take that!'

I rounded the horse-box to see a burly man in breeches and riding boots striking Scamp's head while my spaniel, gamely refusing to be cowed, tried to bite at the whip to take it from him.

I ran forward and grabbed the man's right arm. So this brute was Moonlight's master! No wonder the policeman had felt sorry for the stallion, knowing that he might have to go back to the circus.

'You leave my dog alone,' I flared. 'You can see Scamp's got spirit and you're out to break it, just as you break the will of the animals in your rotten circus.'

Carl Fossley shook me off. 'If the dog's yours, then keep him under control. I haven't time to waste. I've come to collect my Arab stallion. Where is he? Round here?'

I followed unhappily as he strode across the yard. I had to hold Scamp's collar because he was still growling and straining to get at the bullying circus owner.

Macgregor and Highland Laird put their heads over the half-doors of their loose-boxes to watch. Moonlight's head did not appear as the Arab was tied up to prevent him from undoing the latch of his door again.

'I suppose my horse is in here, sulking because he's got to work for his living again.'

Carl Fossley made for the door of Moonlight's loose-box.

From the corner of my eye, I saw something move in an upstairs window. I turned to see Mrs Duncan in her dressing gown, leaning half-way out of the window. She was gesticulating.

'Just a minute,' she called and Mr Fossley turned to

stare at her. 'I don't want you to take that stallion away. I'll make you an offer for him.'

Carl Fossley goggled at her in surprise. 'This stallion is a valuable liberty horse, madam.' He broke off, and I realised that he had probably heard that Lochside Pony Farm was in financial difficulties. 'I'd want a lot of money for him.'

'How much?' called Mrs Duncan and I could see Carl Fossley's mind working, no doubt wondering just how much money he could get out of her.

'Well, the Strathtay Show is coming up in a few days. No doubt you'll be able to sell one or two of your animals there . . . Shall we say eight hundred pounds?'

I gasped at the amount, but Mrs Duncan never batted an eyelid. 'Done!' she said swiftly. 'But I won't be able to pay you until after the show.'

From inside the loose-box Moonlight had turned his head to look at his former master. His ears were back and I knew he had recognised Carl Fossley and was no doubt recalling earlier ill-treatment. He gave a squeal, tugged at his rope to try to get free, and then began to paw the ground in a threatening way. I saw Carl Fossley's face lose a little of its colour and I knew that he realised Moonlight hated him.

Stallions never forgive a wrong and Moonlight was intent on revenge!

The circus owner seemed to realise that, if he had him back, the stallion might wait his chance to attack.

76

Moonlight might even kill Carl Fossley!

Such things have been known. With all animals there comes a limit to what they will endure. The Arab liberty horse had reached this point where Carl Fossley was concerned and the bully knew it.

'I'll leave him here until after the show,' he told Mrs Duncan hastily, continuing in a blustering way: 'Mind you, if that money isn't forthcoming, then I shall reclaim him immediately.'

When Rob learned of his mother's bargain he was appalled.

'We're never going to be able to raise enough money, Mum. Now that Miss Gordon's nobbled the Maitlands we haven't a hope.'

'Oh, yes, we have,' Mrs Duncan said determinedly. 'The Maitlands told Jackie that they'd be guided by the judges' decision at the Show as to which animals they'd buy. We've got as good a chance as Elspeth Gordon if we work hard.'

'Not without you we haven't, Mum.' Rob was realistic. 'It's your magic touch in the show ring that makes all the difference.'

'Well, I may not be fit enough to cope with the actual exhibiting,' his mother admitted ruefully. 'But there's nothing to stop me passing on to you four all my know-how.' She glanced out of the window to the spring sunshine. 'Put a chair for me in the yard, wrap me up in plenty of rugs and we'll have a full-scale show rehearsal. Each of you can lead round the ponies that you'll be handling at the show. I'll be able to see them, notice any points in grooming and presentation that could be improved and give you some hints on walking them, trotting them and bringing them into the line-up in the best way to catch the judges' gaze.'

13 Pixie's foal

For the next few days we worked hard preparing the mares and foals for the show. Mrs Duncan sat well rugged on a folding chair in the middle of the stable yard as we went through our paces.

She told us how to grasp the head-collars nearer the ponies' jaws and to run at just the right pace to display the ponies' action.

Her keen eyes noticed at once whether anything was wrong. Highland Laird was not picking up his feet. On investigation he proved to have a slight crack in the horn of one of his hooves. So Rob was sent with him at once to the smithy for attention.

On the day before the show we concentrated extra hard on grooming and Mrs Duncan herself levelled the ponies' manes and tails.

On the morning of the great day, tails had to be washed and brushed. Hooves were oiled and all the entrants were finished off with the dandy brush until their coats shone.

We started to load them into the horse-boxes—Lochside's own vehicle, driven by Mr Macpherson, and a couple more which had been hired for the occasion. Then the postman arrived to deliver two letters.

Mrs Duncan's colour heightened when she read the first.

'That wretched Elspeth Gordon!' she exclaimed. 'She's sent this letter to arrive this morning in the hope of rattling me.'

'What does it say?' Rob's arm went protectively around his mother's shoulders.

'It's another of her so-called "offers" to buy Lochside. She points out that it's a particularly fair one as she's named the price before the show. Afterwards, she says, the price could well be lower. She seems sure that with me unable to show the ponies myself, the results are bound to be poor.'

'Charming!' Babs exploded. 'That settles it. We'll show her!'

I felt Fiona's fingers touch mine. 'We jolly well will,' she vowed.

'Miss Gordon wants me to phone her right away to let her know if I accept her offer,' Mrs Duncan went on.

'So what are you going to do, Mum?' Rob asked anxiously.

Mrs Duncan's mouth set firmly. 'I shall do nothing, of course. I shan't even bother to phone. Elspeth Gordon's offer's beneath contempt.'

'You're sure you're doing the right thing, Mum?' Rob's eyes were worried. 'It won't be too much for you, after your accident, to carry on running the pony farm, will it?'

'Of course it won't,' Mrs Duncan said briskly.' Only

yesterday Doctor McLean admitted that I'd made good progress since I discharged myself from hospital. All I need are one or two wins to complete the cure.'

'And some sales to the Maitlands,' added Babs. 'What's in your other letter, Mrs Duncan?'

Rob's mother looked puzzledly at the scrawled untidy handwriting on the second envelope. Her bafflement changed to concern as she read the contents.

'It's from Carl Fossley,' she told us, 'reminding me of his deal. He says that he's had an offer from a foreign circus to buy Moonlight, and that he'll be at the show and that he'll be coming here immediately afterwards to claim either his cheque or the stallion.'

'Oh, dear!' I sighed.

We all exchanged unhappy glances. So much depended on the results of the show. The fate of Lochside Pony Farm and the Highland ponies belonging to the stud; Mrs Duncan's and Rob's future; and now the fate of Moonlight.

The thought of the Arab stallion returning to Carl Fossley had been bad enough. The idea of him going to some foreign circus was unbearable!

Rob and his mother left for the showground in the first horse-box with Macgregor and Highland Laird. Babs and Fiona followed in the second with Cloud and Heather Belle and their foals. I accompanied a young driver called Jock Fyfe in the third horse-box with Tiptree and Pixie, the mare who had 'borrowed'

Cloud's foal but had not yet had her own.

It was when we were about two miles from Strath-tay that I heard ominous noises from the back of the horse-box. It sounded as though one of the mares was trying to kick down the partition.

'Better pull up,' I groaned to Jock Fyfe. 'It could be trouble.'

We jumped down from the cab and ran round to the back of the horse-box, letting down the ramp to look anxiously inside. From one division Tiptoes turned her head and whinnied, glad to see us, evidently thinking that we had reached our destination and were about to let her out.

'No, Tiptoes!' I told her. 'We're not there yet.'

Giving her a friendly pat on the rump. I climbed into Pixie's compartment. The dun mare seemed distressed. She had evidently tried to lie down in the narrow space, but fortunately found it impossible. She was now leaning heavily, sides bulging, half wedged against the partition. Her flanks were heaving and, as she turned her head towards us, I could see that her eyes were glassy and her nostrils flaring.

'Good gracious!' I gasped and I'm sure I sounded as alarmed as I felt. 'She is about to have her foal! And Mrs Duncan said she wouldn't foal for a fortnight or more. Oh gosh! Now she'll be out of the show. And so will Tiptoes. We'll have to stay here until the foal is born and just hope that everything goes well.'

Jock joined me in the back of the horse-box. Fortunately he seemed to know about ponies and, as he examined Pixie, his homely Scots voice and gentle touch seemed to reassure her.

'We'd better get the mare out of the van,' he decided, encouraging Pixie to stand firmly on her feet and backing her gently towards the ramp. 'Come on, lassie. Easy does it. There you are, now. That's a good lass.'

Jock soon had her safely on the grass at the road-side. Then he backed the horse-box alongside to shelter her and unfolded a large tarpaulin to make a screen.

'That'll make her feel a wee bitty safer,' he explained. 'Mebbe she'll think she's in a sort of stable . . . Now, Jackie, you run along to the phone box at

the next cross-roads and let Mrs Duncan and Rob know what's happening. Ask the operator to put you through to the show ground. There'll be a temporary line ... Here,' he called after me as I set off, 'let's check that you've got enough change.'

Soon I was in the phone box, breathlessly talking to one of the stewards. He said he couldn't get hold of Mrs Duncan just then because she was in the collecting ring with Rob and Macgregor. So I left a message before hurrying back to the horse-box and Pixie.

'Any news yet?' I gasped as Jock emerged from behind the tarpaulin.

He shook his head. 'Mares can't be hurried. It'll be a wee while yet, I'm thinking.'

'Oh, dear! And there's nothing we can do about it.'
I sighed. 'It's another fifteen miles to the show ground,
so it's no use my trying to lead Tiptoes. We'll just have
to make up our minds that both Tiptoes and Pixie will
be out of the show.'

What was happening at the show ground, I wondered? At this moment Macgregor and Highland
Laird were probably being judged for the stallion
championship. Next, Babs and Fiona would be showing Cloud and Heather Belle and their foals. All the
Lochside ponies needed to take first or second prize in
order to make up for the fact that the entries of the
other two mares would have to be scrapped.

It seemed as though I sat by the horse-box, gazing
at the tarpaulin, for hours, listening to Jock encouraging Pixie and answering the queries of motorists and
others who pulled up and had to be discouraged from
trying to 'help'.

It wasn't until three-quarters of an hour after
midday that the foal arrived. Jock shouted the good
news from behind the horse-box.

Then, a little later, he called me to see the newly-
born filly.

She was dark brown with long white 'stockings' on
her back legs and short white 'socks' on her front ones.
She was a little beauty, and I knew that Mrs Duncan
and Rob would be pleased with her.

Already the foal was standing up, flicking her tail
and trying to feed while Pixie nuzzled her lovingly.

After about half-an-hour Jock decided that the

mother and daughter could be moved. He carried the foal into the horse-box, its long legs dangling, while Pixie followed anxiously. I stayed in the back with them while Jock drove carefully, going slowly so as not to shake or bump his youngest passenger.

It was three o'clock when we reached the show ground!

14 No prizes for Lochside

As soon as Jock pulled up on the show ground and let down the ramp, I caught sight of Mrs Duncan and Fiona standing glumly beside the Lochside horse-box. I knew right away that something was wrong.

One look at Mrs Duncan's face was enough to tell me that they'd had bad luck and that the shock of whatever had happened had made her feel poorly again.

'Rob's looking for the doctor,' Babs announced.

'Not that there's any need,' Mrs Duncan said quickly, wiping a hand across her brow and trying to stand up. 'I'll be well enough in a minute or two when I've had time to get used to the idea of having to leave Lochside.'

That could only mean one thing!

'So Miss Gordon's ponies beat yours?' I queried gently.

Mrs Duncan nodded. 'Macgregor went lame.'

'Highland Laird played up,' added Fiona.

'And that horrid Elspeth Gordon, backed one of her mares into Cloud,' Babs added. 'Cloud lashed out to defend her foal and got sent out of the ring.'

'And what happened to Heather Belle?' I groaned.

'Oh, need we go into all that?' Mrs Duncan sighed wearily. 'Let's try to put it all behind us and have a look at the new arrival.'

Followed by Fiona, Babs and she walked gamely to the horse-box to gaze at Pixie's foal.

One thought was in all our minds.

The Strathtay Show had been a disaster as far as Lochside Pony Farm was concerned. The stud would be sold. Laird of Lochside, Heather Belle's foal and Pixie's little filly would grow up somewhere else. Whether Rob's mother decided to sell to Elspeth Gordon or some other buyer, her's and Rob's happy pony-owning days were over. As for Moonlight there was no hope of saving the Arab stallion. Carl Fossley would ship him off to the foreign circus and there was nothing any of us could do about it.

'I suppose there's no hope that the Maitlands might still want to buy any of the Lochside ponies?' I hazarded to Rob while the show ground doctor was examining his mother.

'Not a chance.' Rob jerked his head across the car park where Herman and Cora Maitland were standing with Elspeth Gordon. 'Look!'

Above their heads, pinned to the side of one of Elspeth Gordon's horse-boxes were seven large rosettes, five reds and two blues.

'Makes you sick doesn't it?' Rob said bitterly as the Maitlands shook hands with Elspeth Gordon, laughing and congratulating her.

'Just look at the sly thing!' exclaimed Babs. 'There she is, pretending to be all modest and charming while Cora Maitland pats her on the back.'

As we watched Elspeth Gordon put her arms round Cora Maitland and kissed her while Mr Maitland made notes on his programme as if jotting down which of Elspeth Gordon's pones he intended to buy.

Rob turned away. 'I can't bear to look any longer.'

Meanwhile Mrs Duncan, having managed to convince the doctor that she was suffering from nothing worse than tiredness and disappointment, walked unsteadily to join us.

At that moment there was one of those meaningful silences that sometimes fall over the noisiest throng. Then I shuddered in anger as I heard Elspeth Gordon give a falsely silvery laugh and say syrupily: 'I'm proud to think my ponies will be going to form part of your New Jersey stud, Cora.'

I turned to see if Mrs Duncan had heard. Rob's mother was looking dreadful but, when she saw that I was watching her, she seemed to pull herself together.

'Come on, everybody! Stop looking so tragic. Mrs Maitland's coming this way. Show her we can be good losers.'

Cora Maitland came steadily towards us, her naturally happy smile replaced by an expression of embarrassed concern.

She shook hands with Mrs Duncan. 'I felt I must just have a word with you before we leave . . . It's a pity your ponies didn't get placed higher in the ring, but then the competition was so keen. Herman and I never realised that Miss Gordon had such first-rate stock.' She glanced over her shoulder as if wondering why her husband had not followed her. 'Talking of Herman, where can he be? Don't say he's gone back to that refreshment tent!' She gave an indulgent laugh. 'It seems he's fallen for your British stone-ginger beer. I wouldn't like to count how many bottles he's drunk today.'

As Mrs Maitland glanced towards the refreshment tent we saw Elspeth Gordon coming out of it. Her face was flushed as though she'd been having a celebratory drink. She saw us looking towards her and waved. Then she started to walk in our direction.

With a sweet smile at Cora Maitland, she turned gloatingly to Rob's mother.

'Well, you've only yourself to blame, Isabel! It was obvious from the beginning that there wouldn't be room for the two of us. One of us had to go to the wall and I should think it was perfectly clear that it wouldn't be me . . . You must have had my letter this morning making a perfectly good offer for Lochside . . . Oh, it's no use your asking me to repeat it now. As I forecast, your poor showing today has knocked hundreds of pounds off the value of your stock. Your ponies will have to come under the hammer.'

I couldn't stand any more. Disregarding Mrs Duncan's warning look, I plunged into battle. 'Yes, that's just what you're hoping for, isn't it? You know very well that the Lochside stock ponies are super and you want to buy them for a song. You're *horrid*!'

Elspeth Gordon's flush deepened. 'Well, after holding out the hand of friendship!' she exclaimed. 'I refuse to stay here and be insulted.'

'Then why don't you go away?' Babs put in frankly.

Elspeth Gordon looked as though she was about to stride off when Mr Maitland appeared at the front of the refreshment tent. The American pony breeder was frowning and looking strangely serious. He held a slip of blue paper in his right hand and was staring around as though he was looking for someone.

'Ah, there you are!' Elspeth Gordon's voice changed to honeyed sweetness as she saw him. 'Are you looking for me?' Then as a taunting aside to us, she added: 'Mr Maitland's buying seven mares from me, you know, and here he is – cheque in hand.'

She glanced from one to the other of us still gloating. She was enjoying every moment.

This was our supreme humiliation. Elspeth was about to be presented with a small fortune before our eyes. This would mean that she could buy up the Lochside Pony Farm at auction and hardly notice she had spent the money!

15   Climax

As Mr Maitland got nearer, I noticed that his expression seemed quite pained. What could be wrong?

Elspeth Gordon was so full of herself, however, that she didn't seem to notice anything odd. Mrs Maitland noticed, though.

'What's cooking, Herman? You look like thunder.'

'I feel like it!' her husband grunted. He moved to stand in front of Miss Gordon and held the cheque in front of her face.

'See this,' he challenged. 'It's drawn on the Chase National Bank and made out to you for fourteen thousand dollars. I was just about to give it to you. But I've changed my mind. Now I'm going to do something else with it.'

Elspeth Gordon looked flabbergasted, but Babs caught at my hand in delight, realising that something sensational was about to happen.

She wasn't disappointed!

We gazed in surprised silence while Mr Maitland waved the cheque slowly in front of Elspeth Gordon's face. Then he said pointedly: 'Yes, Miss Gordon. This is what I'm going to do with the cheque.'

As we watched he slowly tore it up!

Fiona caught my other hand as the torn-up cheque fluttered into the litter bin.

This was wonderful!

Rob and Mrs Duncan seemed to think so, too. Their faces were enraptured.

I turned to Elspeth Gordon. She was still looking astonished.

'Is this some kind of joke, Mr Maitland?' Her voice was now rather shrill. 'You're surely not running out on your bargain.' She glanced accusingly at the rest of us. 'Has some person here been making mischief?'

'You can say that again, Miss Gordon.' Mr Maitland's words were slow and deliberate. 'Somebody *has* made mischief and that somebody, ma'am, is you. It's no good your denying it because I heard it all with my own ears. I was right there in the refreshment tent enjoying a last bottle of British stone-ginger. You couldn't see me, because the table at which I was sitting was right behind a stack of crates. But I heard you all right. You were telling the steward that you were having a "wee drappie" to celebrate your victory over these good people here.'

Our ears flapped. Cora Maitland's jaw dropped and she gaped at her husband.

Now our curiosity was at fever pitch. Just what had Elspeth Gordon said to have made Mr Maitland so angry? She was guilty, sure enough. It was written all over her now heavily flushed face. Not, even she, with all her self-possession, could pick up this cart-load of bricks she had evidently so heavily dropped.

'I'm so sorry, Mr Maitland,' she tried apologising. 'Whatever it was that I said to the steward, I do regret and I really do apologise.'

'I doubt the sincerity of any apology you could offer, Miss Gordon.' He turned on his heel. 'I think we've said enough to each other. Good day.'

Realising that everything was lost, Elspeth Gordon let him see the true side of her malicious nature. 'You Americans!' she shrilled after him. 'You're impossible! Even with your dollars falling you think everybody's dependent on you. Well, let me tell you, we're not! I'm glad to think I'll now be able to sell my ponies to really knowledgeable pony breeders and not to a couple who are so influenced by a few rosettes.'

'Just what does she mean by that?' Cora Maitland turned to her husband, as we all walked away.

Her husband put an arm protectively round her shoulders. 'I guess we let ourselves be a mite carried away by all the excitement of this Scottish show.'

Cora Maitland nodded.

'All those skirling pipers and the judges – and the Scottish aristocracy handing out rosettes. I suppose it did kind of make us feel Miss Gordon's ponies must be the best in the world to merit such a fuss.'

'Yeah!' Herman Maitland nodded ruefully. 'But we should have known better.' He groaned. 'What kind of pony breeder am I, to let myself be influenced by a few trappings? It makes me feel that Miss Gordon was right in what she said to the steward.'

'Just what did she say?' Babs asked bluntly.

'She was bragging to the steward that she'd made a killing, sold seven ponies for nearly double their worth to a couple of loaded Yankees who didn't know one end of a pony from another. She said that if she hadn't helped her own luck along by managing to upset one of your mares in the ring – at least one of the prizes would have gone to Lochside and then I might have decided to buy from you as well.'

'That's true, you know,' Rob pointed out. 'Lochside ponies are just as good as Elspeth Gordon's, any day.'

'Some of them are a lot better,' Babs said loyally. 'It's just that the luck of the show went Elspeth Gordon's way today.'

'And I was fool enough to be influenced by it!' Mr Maitland turned to Rob. 'I guess I was biased, too, by that letter you wrote me, young man . . . I thought it was a mighty poor example of your British fair play for you to run down a rival, warning me against Miss Gordon in that way.'

'But you can see why he did it now, Herman, can't you?' Cora Maitland asked.

'Sure. He just wanted to put me wise,' Herman said before turning to Rob. 'I reckon I owe you an apology, young man, and to show that I mean it I'll write another cheque – this time made out to your mother.' He turned to Mrs Duncan. 'Just which of your mares and foals are you prepared to sell me, ma'am?'

'The best way to settle that, Mr Maitland,' Mrs Duncan smiled in a relaxed way for the first time, 'would be for you and your wife to follow us back to Lochside Pony Farm. Then, you can inspect all the stock and decide for yourself which of the ponies you want to buy.'

'Away from the influence of the show ring, honey.' Cora Maitland tucked her hand through her husband's arm. 'That sounds like a fair idea to me.'

'And to us!' Fiona agreed whole-heartedly, before breaking into a run. 'Jackie, Babs and I will hurry back and get a meal ready while you're deciding on the details. We'll make it a real celebration high-tea.'

16   Ponies for ever

Back at Lochside Pony Farm, the Maitlands helped us to lead the ponies out of the vans.

Then they began a tour of the fields with Rob to see all the animals. Suddenly we heard a heavy vehicle lumbering up the lane, and a Fossley circus van rumbled into the yard.

Scamp gave a low growl and I had to grab his collar as Carl Fossley jumped out of the cab and blustered to Moonlight's loose-box.

Mrs Duncan was resting inside but she must have heard the vehicle and guessed what its arrival meant because she put her head through the open bedroom window to call down: 'Where do you think you're going, Mr Fossley?'

'I intend to claim my stallion before he's seized with the rest of your assets.' Contempt was plain in the look Carl Fossley gave Rob's mother. 'According to what some of the folks were saying at the show, there'll be a bankruptcy order any day now.'

'Says who?' Mr Maitland moved to stand in front of him challengingly. Beside the circus bully the American looked small, but lack of height in no way lessened Mr Maitland's authority. 'I warn you to be careful what you say about Mrs Duncan's financial position,' he went on firmly. 'There's no question of Lochside Pony Farm being insolvent. Mrs Duncan and I are just about to complete a deal which will ensure that her credit's good for a long time to come.'

'In that case, I'll have my money and leave the stallion here.' Carl Fossley's raised voice reached Mrs Duncan at the window. 'My price has gone up since this morning, missis. The foreign circus owner wired a message increasing his offer to a thousand pounds.'

While Mrs Duncan was hurrying downstairs, Mr Maitland drew his cheque book from his pocket. 'I'll pay you the money on Mrs Duncan's behalf right away.'

'I can't let you do that,' Mrs Duncan protested.

'Nonsense! Mr Maitland said briskly. 'It'll give me great pleasure to send this man packing.'

'In that case,' said Rob, 'you must be sure to deduct the amount of Moonlight's purchase from the cheque when the deals are completed.'

'We'll talk about that later,' Mr Maitland said. 'As a matter of fact, I was thinking that an Arab stallion's not much use to you on a Highland pony stud . . .'

'But we could use him in New Jersey.' His wife was quick to follow his train of thought. She turned to Mrs Duncan. 'You see, honey, Herman and I breed Welsh ponies as well as Highland ponies, so I guess a dash of pure Arab would be just the thing to improve the line.'

'Very nice for you, I'm sure,' interjected Carl Fossley. 'But all I want is my money.' He jerked his

99

head at Herman Maitland. 'Just make out the cheque, mister, and I'll be off.'

'Before you go, Mr Fossley,' Rob put in quickly, 'there's something you should know. A senior RSPCA inspector was at the show, so I took the opportunity of having a word with him.' He glanced towards his mother. 'I didn't tell you, Mum, but after Mr Fossley's visit the other day I wrote a letter to the RSPCA putting them in the picture about the way he seems to handle his animals. The inspector said they'd had several complaints about Fossley's. Already two RSPCA men have visited the circus, around the counties, and made suggestions for the improved comfort and well-being of the animals. Apparently they've issued several warnings. Well . . .' he gazed directly into Carl Fossley's eyes, 'it seems there won't be any more warnings. Next time, the RSPCA are going to add a prosecution to the two you've already had through the police.'

'So you'd better mend your ways, Mr Fossley,' added Babs.

'And so say all of us,' added Mr Maitland. 'Cora and I hate cruelty. So just as soon as we get to London, we'll be calling at the RSPCA headquarters to give them a donation and make sure this thing's followed through.' His gaze seemed to bore right through the circus owner. 'If you don't treat your animals better, your circus will be closed down.'

'Then you'll be the one with the shaky credit, Mr Fossley.' I couldn't resist adding. 'Serve you right!'

An hour-and-a-half later we were sitting round the big table in the farm kitchen, starting on the gigantic meal that Babs and I had helped Fiona to prepare.

There were bowls of salad with lettuce, cucumber, tomatoes, hard-boiled eggs and grated carrot; sliced ham, tongue and cold chicken, fresh baked scones to be eaten with Mrs Duncan's home-made strawberry jam. Then bottled pears from the farm larder, with lashings of creamy custard, completed the feast.

'Before we start I'd like to seal the bargain, Mrs Duncan.' Mr Maitland again had his cheque book in his hand. 'There will be the four mares and foals, two fillies and the yearling colt, as well as Moonlight that I'll be taking across the Atlantic, and I'd like to enter into a contract to buy another four fillies next year. Shall we say twenty four thousand dollars in all?'

'That's a fortune,' Fiona gasped.

'Not quite, honey, not in these inflationary times,' Mrs Maitland smiled, 'but it'll keep your aunt's pony farm going for a while, I guess, and give her time to get back her health and strength.'

'I'll do that all right.' Mrs Duncan laid her hand warmly on the arm of her new friend. 'Cora, my dear, I feel better already.'

'Hurray!' said Babs. 'Then this can be a proper celebration!'

'To be sealed with a drink.' Rob signalled to me and Fiona. Fiona helped Rob to carry in a crate of stone-ginger beer that had been standing in the cool of the larder while I brought tall glasses from the dresser.

'Ginger beer from a stone bottle, Mr Maitland.' He poured out a frothing glass. 'We bought a crateful specially for you.'

'What could be more appropriate?' said Babs. 'If it hadn't been for Mr Maitland's taking such a liking to stone-ginger, he wouldn't have been in the refreshment tent to hear Elspeth Gordon reveal herself as a rival in her true colours.'

'And Rob and I would have had to give up Lochside!' Mrs Duncan said feelingly. 'It seems fate must have been on our side after all.'

'Right has a way of triumphing in the end, honey.' Cora Maitland patted her hand.

And so it did, I thought, even though there were times when one might never believe it.

Rob and his mother deserved their good fortune. They'd worked so hard; they'd always looked after their ponies and young stock; and even when bad luck seemed to pile up against them, they'd still tried to do the right thing by Moonlight, staking their last pounds in a desperate bid to save him from Carl Fossley's callous plan.

Now things had gone right for them . . . and Moonlight. The Arab stallion would be going to a luxurious home in New Jersey with the mares, foals and yearlings for which Herman Maitland had just paid.

Here in Scotland, Macgregor, Highland Laird, Cloud and her foal, Pixie and Heather Belle would graze the Lochside meadows and roam the heather-clad hills, happy and secure with Mrs Duncan and Rob as their caring owners.

Yes, we really had something to celebrate!